CLB 2230
© 1988 Colour Library Books Ltd, Godalming, Surrey, England.
All rights reserved.
Printed and bound in Hong Kong by Leefung Asco Printers Ltd.
ISBN 0 86283 640 9

THE
WILD LANDSCAPES OF
AUSTRALIA

COLOUR LIBRARY BOOKS

As long ago as the 14th century, Chinese geographers pondered upon the nature of lands which they felt undoubtedly lay to the south of the islands of Timor and Java. Some of these scholars thought that a kingdom populated only by women lay there awaiting the intrepid explorer and, no doubt, that might have prompted a rush of bold youths intent on discovering Australia. Perhaps it was because other Chinese wise men stated that only Wei-lu – the great hole into which the waters of the world drained in mighty flood – lay there to suck them down to early death, that no serious attempts were made to cross the seas to find out what lay beyond the glimmering horizon.

The history of exploration has always comprised a strange combination of a quest for adventure and a desire for riches. Centuries ago, men from the great seafaring nations of Europe ranged far across the oceans in a search for opportunities in distant markets, and raw materials and minerals. A revival in the study of ancient Greek writings had revealed to medieval man the works of Ptolemy. In his work *Guide to Geography*, he suggested that the Indian Ocean was bounded by a southern continent. This made sense to any reasonable man who believed in a round world, for would not the unbalanced weight of Europe in the northern hemisphere otherwise topple the whole planet?

So the tall-masted ships sailed away, seeking fame, fortune and *Terra Australis Incognita* – the unknown southern land. The Dutch were one of the main trading nations of Europe and, in 1611, Hendrik de Brouwer discovered that if he wished to get to the Spice Islands, the Moluccas of the East Indies, ahead of ships from rival nations, he only had to head directly east after rounding the Cape of Good Hope instead of sailing north towards India first. Then the Roaring Forties would sweep him towards his goal. However, he had to head north at the right moment in order to reach safe harbour in Java. Because of the hopelessly inaccurate maps which were then. in existence, Dutch navigators – following de Brouwer's route – neglected to head at the appropriate time and, as a result, many sailors had the dubious pleasure of becoming the first white travelle to be wrecked off Austrlia. Today, the wrecks of several ships from this era are known to lie off Western Australia deep down in Davy Jones's locker.

Accounts of Australia's landscapes from early Dutch sailors did little to encourage others. In 1623, Jan Carstens surveyed the Gulf of Carpentaria and wrote of the land he had seen, 'We saw no fruit-bearing tree, and nothing that man could make use of. In our judgement, it is the most arid and barren region on earth.'

The British, however, felt that Australia could be very useful to them and started to send convicts to settle there. When the men from the First Fleet landed at Botany Bay in January 1788, it was intended that they should be self-sufficient as regards food. On their first day they found poor soil, a poor harbour and a lack of drinking water. Hardship stared them straight in the face and the settlers who followed often fared little better in a land which often appeared pitilessly inhospitable.

Perhaps it was the more fanciful accounts, or at least the most optimistic of men, that helped maintain the flow of those who wished to see what lay over the next horizon. One man who had sailed to Australia, John Lort Stokes – Captain of *HMS Beagle* – wrote in 1841, 'I could not refrain from breathing a prayer that ere long the now level horizon would be broken by a succession of tapering spires rising from the many Christian hamlets that must ultimately stud this country.'

In the very same year that Stokes propounded his vision for the future, at the other side of the continent, a young Englishman by the name of Edward John Eyre struck out to find rich grazing land for the fledgling, five-year-old colony of South Australia. He set out from Fowlers Bay on horseback with four companions, and with them went the high hopes of all people that they would find the golden plains of milk and honey which were thought to exist nearby. The land Eyre was crossing was the Nullarbor Plain; vast, waterless, treeless – it staggers the human imagination. The local Aborigines knew that there was no water there. All that awaited the foolish was Jeedara, the giant serpent, who lived in the caves beneath the limestone plain. It could often be heard at blowholes hissing and roaring in black anger as it slid back from the sea, eager to take the next unwary victim upon the barren plain. Perhaps the Aborigines were right, for five months later Eyre staggered into the town of Albany with only one remaining companion. It was just as everyone had feared in their worst

Facing page: a rock formation known as the Loop, in Kalbarri National Park.

dreams. The country was a wild and savage place with a merciless terrain.

However, in 1875, another man decided to travel a little further and see for himself what lay in the sandy wastes. He was to show others how to survive successfully in the harsh interior, even though he discovered no verdant pastures there. Ernest Giles made use of camels on his journeys, being so impressed by their hardiness that he even wrote poems in praise of them:

'Though the scrubs may range around me
My camel shall bear me on,
Though the desert may surround me,
It hath springs that shall be won.'

From Fowlers Bay, he went to the gathering place of the Aboriginal tribes at Youldeh, where the magical underground river, Yooldil Gabbi, surfaced as a fresh spring. After he left there he wrote, 'My caravan departed in a long single string to the North, and Youldeh and the place therof knew us no more.' Warned by the Aborigines that this well was the only known water supply on the Nullarbor Plain, he went to the rockhole called Ooldabinna, where he had been told that water would be available.

Beyond Ooldabinna, his party found water at Boundary Dam, but it was seventeen days before they managed to reach any other supply again. Of the lands he traversed he wrote, 'The silence and the solitude of this mighty waste was appalling to the mind...' and of the waterhole they eventually discovered, which saved their lives, he wrote in his diary, 'I venture to dedicate it to our most gracious Queen. The great desert in which I found it, and which will probably extend to the west as far as it does to the east, I have also honoured with Her Majesty's mighty name, calling it the Great Victoria Desert, and the spring Queen Victoria's Spring. In future times, these may be celebrated localities in the British Monarch's dominions. I have no Tanganyikas, Lualabas or Zambezis, like the great African travellers, to honour with Her Majesty's name, but the humble offering of a little spring in a hideous desert.'

This seems to echo the thoughts of most of these early explorers. They sought the chivalrous quest of adventure, but they also wanted good land or maybe some more tangible, material wealth such as gold. What they found instead was endless miles of desert and a land which seemed determined to snuff out their very existence. No wonder they could not wax lyrical about it. As the explorer R.T. Maurice said in 1900, 'Any man who would travel this country for pleasure would go to Hell for a pastime.' Today, perhaps we can reflect with Daisy Bates on other aspects of Australia's landscape which still strike a chord with people who live in a highly urbanised society: 'It takes some time for the beauty of the open places to reach one's soul, but once there, hills, sea, river, wood, all are as nothing beside the beauty of the flat land that goes on and on in infinite open space from sunrise to glorious sunset.'

What was it that made people stay in Australia, besides those who were sent there in transport ships and did not have the choice? There was, in fact, plenty of wealth to be obtained if one did not wander off trying to cross the blistering land in search of mythical inland seas and rolling, lush acres. For instance, in 1823, John Oxley – Surveyor-General of New South Wales – explored the Tweed and, being greatly impressed by what he saw, said that the wonderful scenery there stretched, '...for miles along a rich valley clothed with magnificent trees, the beautiful uniformity of which was only interrupted by the turns and windings of the river which here and there appeared like small lakes'. Now that was something that people could understand: timber and water. There was richness in the land, as long as you knew where to look for it.

Although trade with the Mother Country had slumped in the early 1840s because of general economic depression, by 1845 the *Sydney Morning Herald* was able to state that, 'sheep-farming, which two years ago was pronounced on all hands a losing concern, is now the most profitable investment in the country. What with the high character of our tallow and the remunerative prices of our fleece, our pastoral interest – the ruling interest in Australia – was never in a more auspicious position than at the present moment'.

Three years later, Joseph Fowles wrote in *Syndey in 1848* of 'our denizens of the pasture-plains boiling down into tallow sufficient meat, per annum, to feed nearly half a million of persons because we have not mouths to eat it; and our denizens of the city luxuriating in all the delicacies which the well-appointed hotels and restaurants of Sydney provide on the most princely scale'. Certainly it seems that life in the big city was good and the sheep-farming was also doing well. It was about this time that Sydney made a hero out of a man who had braved the interior of the Northern Territory. His journey in 1844-45 had made him an overnight celebrity and, although he had been forced to abandon a second expedition, he set out on a third expedition in 1848...

The idea behind Ludwig Leichhardt's trip was to traverse Australia from east to west, travelling across the northern parts of the continent. Not far from the Gregory River, on the Gregory Downs station, stands an old tree. There, carved into its gnarled trunk, are the letters VI and the initials L.L., with an arrow pointing enigmatically to the northwest. Did this mean that Ludwig Leichhardt intended making his sixth camp to the northwest by the Roper River? Who can tell, for he and his party vanished into the depths of the Gulf Country and into history, never to be seen again by mortal eye.

One man with a dream was Surveyor-General Major Mitchell, who believed that there was a river, 'its course analogous to that of the Amazon's' which would give entry to the heart of the island continent and the rich pastures there. He wrote: 'I felt the ardour of my early youth, when I first sought distinction in the crowded camp and battlefield, revive as I gave loose to my reflections...It seemed that even war and victory, with all their glory, were far less alluring than the pursuit of researches such as these, the objects of which were to spread the light of civilisation over a portion of the globe yet unknown, though rich, perhaps, in the luxuriance of uncultivated nature, and where science might accomplish new and unthought-of dicoveries; while intelligent man would find a region teeming with useful vegetation, abounding with rivers, hills and vallies, and waiting only for his enterprising spirit and improving hand.' He was luckier than many and went on to discover fertile grasslands in the southwest which he called Australia Felix.

Many people, of course, preferred get-rich-quick schemes to sheep-farming or agriculture and the gold rushes were ideal for them. Gold had been found in 1851 and the prosperity of Australia was assured from that time on as a veritable flood of immigrants began to arrive on the scene, bringing skills and labour with their dreams to this land of literally golden opportunities. Not everyone found gold and that left a few people cursing:

'Damn the teamsters, damn the track
Damn Coolgardie there and back
Damn the goldfields, damn the weather
Damn the bloody country altogether.'

Exactly the kind of hardships these men faced when they dared the wild landscape that unfolded before them, was neatly summarised by Martin Walsh when he addressed the Governor at a function in Goldfields: 'Consider the prospector, what he has done for the country. He goes out into the desert with his pick in one hand, his waterbag in the other and his life in the other. He goes where the hand of man has never trod foot, and when he faces the wilderness, the only signs of life that he sees are the bones of the dead men who went before him.' The men who searched for gold knew exactly what might be in store for them when they set out:

'Out on the Western Diggings,
That land of sand and gold
Our plucky lads they ventured
Their lives for wealth untold.
Mothers mourn for manly sons
And wives for husbands dear,
And daughters mourn for sweethearts true,
They'll never more be near.

Onward in the strife for riches,
Onward in the strife for gain,
Surely virgin gold bewitches
But it causes tears and pain.
Many a silent grave it tells
Of the miners' long long rest
While others on the plains are bleaching
Beneath the skies of the Golden West.'

The attempts to discover the secrets of the continent had led to death for many an adventurer, as on the ill-fated expedition of Burke and Wills in 1860. But was there any truth in the idea of an inland sea? Captain Charles Sturt was completely convinced that the hinterland, 'had formerly been an archipelago of islands, and that the apparently boundless plains...were the seabeds of the channels'. In fact, he was partly right, as the interior had once been on the sea floor, but had been laid bare to the sun some 60 million years before. Now the lakes there are dried up and covered with salt, the largest being Lake Eyre.

It was on seeing Lake Eyre and then trying to cross its desolate wastes that many an outback explorer must have wondered about the wisdom of his choice of career. A geologist and explorer who visited the place in 1939, Dr C.T. Madigan, wrote: 'All who have travelled there have felt this haunting sense of desolation and death. The song dies on the drover's lips; silence falls on the exploring party. It is like entering a vast tomb; one hesitates to break the silence. The rivers are dead, the trees are dead, but overshadowing all in the qualities of death is the very heart of the region, the great lake itself, a horrible travesty, a vast, white, prostrate giant of a lake. Here time seems to have stood still for ages, and all is dead...The Dead Heart, the focus of a drainage basin of 450,000 square miles of country will never throb again.'

It turned out that the good doctor was wrong, for a very wet summer in 1949-50 filled the lake with rivers, although these evaporated at the rate of 254cm a year. Then, in 1974, following exceptional rainfall, the water level was up to six metres deep in places and a four-man team in two punts, one of which capsized, made the first recorded crossing by boat of Lake Eyre.

Some 800 kilometres to the northwest of Lake Eyre, two massive outcrops rise out of the desert floor: the Olgas and Ayers Rock. In 1873, William Gosse became the first man to visit the Rock, although it had been sighted by Ernest Giles in 1872. Gosse described in his journal his initial impressions: 'When I was only two miles distant, and the hill for the first time coming into view, what was my astonishment to find it was an immense pebble rising abruptly from the plain. This rock is certainly the most wonderful natural feature...'

William Joy in *The Explorers* said that, 'Well into the 20th Century, one vast area of Australia still defied the explorer. This was the desert later called the Simpson...' Dr Madigan made the first survey flights over the area in 1929 and wrote, 'The whole expanse below was like a pink and gigantic circular gridiron ribbed with close, straight sand ridges from horizon to horizon.' His descriptions led people to say that the desert could never be crossed on foot. But Edmund Colson, who was a settler living at Bloods Creek, a remote settlement west of Oodnadatta, said 'Give me a good season, a blackfellow who'll do what I tell him, and a few good camels and I'll do it myself.' After sixteen days he turned up in Birdsville, to a population who initially could not believe he had accomplished the feat. However, after a few days rest it was time to be going home and Colson saddled up and traversed the Simpson once more on his way back to Bloods Creek.

Dr Madigan eventually conducted his own expedition across the burning sands by camel. The heat that he and others have faced there can be summarised by a description made by a 19th-century naturalist who had captured a blue-tongue skink there in order to examine it: 'Having my hands full of specimens, I asked a blackfellow to look after it and not to let it escape, when to my surprise he simply put it down on the hot sand. It was perfectly alive when he put it down, having been captured in its hole, and when placed on the ground it began to travel at some rate, but after going five yards its movements became slower and slower, and before ten yards had been traversed, they ceased and the animal was quite dead – simply apparently baked to death by contact with the hot sand.'

Even before it was discovered, learned men had debated the existence of a massive landmass in the southern hemisphere. When Australia had been found, explorers sought to prise its secrets from the wild landscape which enveloped them; many died in the attempt. Today, when a large majority of people live in urban communities, the outback still remains; vast and desolate, it is still a frontier for those who seek challenge in their lives.

Facing page: the coastline of Kalbarri National Park.

Lying southwest of the town of Albany in Western Australia, Torndirrup National Park (above and right) is famous for its rugged and romantic coastline. Top: Cape Leeuwin, (facing page top and overleaf left) fine weather at Cape Naturaliste, and (facing page bottom) stalactites in Jewel Cave, all part of beautiful Leeuwin-Naturaliste National Park on the Western Australian seaboard. Overleaf: (right top) Hippo's Yawn and (right bottom) Wave Rock, two aptly-named rock formations near Hyden in the state's wheat-growing belt.

Previous pages: (left) a fire lookout near Manjimup, (right top) soft gold sand at Wayudup, and (right bottom) diamonds of light on the sea at Yallingup, all in Western Australia. Also in this state, midway between Perth and Geraldtown in Nambung National Park, strange rock formations known as the Pinnacles (these pages), legacies of powerful winds, stand in individual saucers of sand.

Hamersley Range National Park (these pages and overleaf left) is one of the largest and finest parks in the state of Western Australia. It covers 617,606 hectares and consists of spectacular mountains and gorges of multi-layered, brightly-coloured rock. Overleaf right: Palm Valley Fauna and Flora Reserve in the Northern Territory, one of the largest and most verdant reserves in the outback.

Facing page: the blood-red rocks of Kelly's Knob Lookout at sunset, (overleaf right) Dales Gorge Lookout, both in Hamersley Range National Park, Western Australia, and (above) part of the state's arid region between the townsite of Wittenoom and Hamersley Gorge. Overleaf left: Ormiston Gorge and part of the huge, rock-rimmed basin known as the Pound in Ormiston Natural Park, Northern Territory.

Top and above: Glen Helen Gorge National Park and its clear pool, and (right) Ellery Creek, a permanent waterhole west of Alice Springs, both close to Ormiston Gorge National Park (facing page) in the Northern Territory. Overleaf: (left) a poinciana tree outside Darwin and (right) birds feeding in the Fogg Dam marshland west of Darwin, in the Northern Territory. Since the dam's construction in the late 1950s, this area has been host to many species of animals and birds.

Above: a saltwater crocodile lurking in the South Alligator River, Kakadu National Park, and (facing page) marshland at Fogg Dam, both in the Northern Territory. Overleaf: (left) sunset heralds a storm near South Alligator River, and (right) clean white sands form the banks of the East Alligator River, west of Darwin in the Northern Territory.

Previous pages: (left) water birds around Fogg Dam, and (right) a saltwater crocodile on the bank of the South Alligator River, Northern Territory. Facing page: sunset in the Northern Territory, where daytime temperatures can remain over 100°F for months, (top) the Makkakai Plains, and (above) the wide expanse of the Adelaide River, all in the Northern Territory.

Both water buffalo (previous pages left), and wild pig (previous pages right) are found in the outback but, having been imported by white settlers, neither are native to Australia. The rounded peaks of the Olgas (facing page) lie to the west of Ayers Rock (above), near Alice Springs in the Northern Territory. These monoliths are the most famous symbols of the 'Red Centre'.

Both the Olgas (previous pages, these pages and overleaf right) and Ayers Rock (above and overleaf left) change colour in varying strengths of sunlight. This phenomenon adds to the mystique surrounding the monoliths, an integral part of Aborigine legend for centuries. Today both remarkable features are protected in Uluru National Park – named after the Aboriginal title for Ayers Rock in recognition of the region's significance for several Aborigine tribes.

Above: a relentlessly-straight road across the outback beyond the small town of Penong, and (facing page) sheep scratch a living on the Eyre Peninsula, South Australia.

Perfectly-maintained, the Eyre Highway (facing page) stretches far across the
South Australia outback. This route is an important lifeline for the state's
more remote coastal regions, connecting Port Augusta, at the head of Spencer
Gulf in South Australia, to Norseman in Western Australia – an overall
distance of approximately two thousand kilometres. Above: a herd of sleek bay
horses on the Eyre Peninsula.

Previous pages: (left) kangaroos, common in the scrubland (right) of the South
Australian outback. Above: part of Wilpena Pound in Flinders Ranges National Park,
South Australia. The aboriginal word *wilpena* means bent fingers, and aptly
describes the pound's resemblance to a cupped hand. Facing page: autumn colours,
some of the loveliest in South Australia's Willowie Forest Reserve.

Previous pages: (left) rich pasture and (right) fertile arable land in Barossa Valley, north of Adelaide in South Australia. In the last century, this valley was settled by people from Silesia and Prussia, and today their legacy of wine-making skills is responsible for the area's internationally-acclaimed vineyards. Above: flowers near Port Wakefield and (facing page) countryside on the Yorke Peninsula, South Australia.

Previous pages: peaceful pastoral scenes in the Barossa Valley, South
Australia. Facing page: the tall rock stacks known as the Twelve Apostles, and
(above and overleaf left) spectacular Island Archway, both on the treacherous,
beautiful coastline of Port Campbell National Park in Victoria. Overleaf right:
sunset at the Crags, a romantic spot on the shoreline between Port Fairy and
Yambuck in Victoria.

Victoria's Grampian Mountains provide excellent mountain and bush walks, some of the finest of which include the fast-flowing McKenzie River (facing page) and the McKenzie River Falls (above). Overleaf: (left) a ploughed field off the state's Calder Highway, and (right) some of the 22,500 hectares of irrigated vineyards around Mildura in north Victoria.

Facing page: the Nobbies, on the most westernmost tip of Phillip Island, and (overleaf left)
Pyramid Rock in the south of the island. Above: a ripe crop awaiting harvest close to Merrijig,
a town near the Great Dividing Range, and (overleaf right) aptly-named Squeaky Beach in
Wilsons Promontory National Park, Victoria, where the sand squeaks underfoot.

Previous pages: (left) sunset over Lake Hume, a large and beautiful lake that spans the Victoria-New South Wales border, and (right) water lilies in San Remo, one of Victoria's fishing villages. Facing page: Whisky Bay and (above) Norman Bay in Wilsons Promontory National Park, Victoria, affectionately called 'The Prom' by locals.

Facing page: a speedboat skims the foreshore at Seaspray on Ninety Mile Beach, Victoria, while (below) the paddle steamer *Coonawarra* slowly noses her way up the great Murray River on the New South Wales-Victoria border. Overleaf: (left) the *Pride of the Murray* paddle steamer on the Murray River at Echuca, and (right) the Kiewa River at Falls Creek, Victoria.

Facing page: sunset silhouettes a lone tree in Stratford Highway Park, Sale, and (above) a deep blue sky dominates the land beside the Gippsland Highway near Stradbroke, both in Victoria. Overleaf: (left) agricultural land seen from the Maroondah Highway near Healesville, and (right) a sunset of deep blues and pinks near the Howqua River, Victoria.

The elegant Tasman Bridge (facing page) links the Tasmanian capital of Hobart with its suburbs. On the Tasman Peninsula, to the southeast of the city, lie several spectacular cliff formations, the Devil's Kitchen (above) being one.

Above: the Tasman Arch, one of the fine cliff formations on the Tasman Peninsula, and (facing page) fertile farmland, plentiful around the town of Ouse, inland from Hobart, Tasmania.

Facing page: skeletons of trees beside Lake Eucumbene, New South Wales, and (below) a hang-glider over Stanwell Park, one of the state's most famous shorelines. Overleaf left: skiing in Perisher Valley in the south of the state, close to Mount Kosciusko, Australia's highest mountain. Overleaf right: Menindee Lake in Kinchega National Park, New South Wales.

The scrubland (these pages) in the outback around Broken Hill, New South Wales, is dry and apparently worthless to man. Yet this land, though infertile, is rich in minerals. Broken Hill itself is built beside the largest silver-lead-zinc deposit in the world, and two million tonnes of ore are mined from the town's environs each year.

Facing page: the course of a dry riverbed remains outlined by trees and shrubs in the arid land between the mining town of Broken Hill, New South Wales, and White Cliffs, a rich opal field to the northeast. Predictably, man's search for opals has pock-marked the White Cliffs area with mines (below).

Previous pages: (left) Menindee Lake, part of the irrigation system for Broken Hill in western New South Wales, and (right) sunset over the state's Barrier Highway. At 275 metres high, Wentworth Falls (facing page and above) are the highest in New South Wales' Blue Mountains National Park and are best viewed from the Scenic Skyway (top). Right: the park's Weeping Rock.

Previous pages: (left) sand strewn with kelp on Shelly Beach, Port Macquarie, and (right) the magnificent cascade of Ellenborough Falls, north of Wingham, both in New South Wales. Facing page: a glorious sweep of sand at Coffs Harbour, the 'Banana Capital', north of the coastal resort of Port Macquarie, New South Wales. Port Macquarie's beaches (above) are popular for their surf and excellent fishing and, not surprisingly, it has become a renowned holiday centre.

Facing page: the spectacular sandstone cliffs of North Head at the northern edge of
Port Jackson, near Sydney, and (above) a multitude of tropical plants in Rainforest
Gully, part of the National Botanic Gardens in Canberra.

Queensland's tropical rainforest, a feature of several national parks, is particularly
beautiful around Lamington National Park's Nagarijoon Falls (previous pages left)
and in Joalah National Park (previous pages right). Above: the distinctive peaks of
Queensland's mounts Beerwah and Coonowrin, and (facing page) one of the state's
famed sunsets over Noosa, the Sunshine Coast's most northerly point.

Previous pages: the deep orange glow of sunset over Fairbairn Reservoir (left), near Emerald in Queensland, contrasts with the verdant Moss Garden (right) of the state's Carnarvon Gorge National Park, south of Springsure. The splendid beaches of Queensland are world-renowned. Stretching for mile after sunny mile and rarely crowded, they are particularly inviting in the Cairns area (above) of the state. A typical Cairns beach, Four Mile Beach (facing page), south of Port Douglas, attracts sunlovers annually for surfing, fishing and, of course, sunbathing on the fine white sands.

As the most northerly city in Queensland, the countryside (previous pages) around Cairns is tropical. Conditions here are ideal for the cultivation of sugar cane, a process which requires firing the canefields (facing page) prior to harvest. Below: cotton fields at Emerald, Queensland.

Previous pages: (left) safe harbour for a yacht near Yorkeys Knob, north of Cairns in Queensland, and (right) the extensive Narinda Tea Plantation, one of many in this state. Queensland exports a wide variety of commodities, including sugar and tropical fruits. Facing page: a Queensland banana plantation, and (above) hoeing sugar cane growing in the state's rich soil.

Previous pages left: a tropical Queensland river. In such a vast state, the maintenance of adequate road and telephone networks (previous pages right) is vital. These pages and overleaf: spectacular islands of the Great Barrier Reef, whose unique beauty stretches for 2,000 kilometres along Australia's northeast coast.